How to Analyze People

System For Analyzing Human Behavior, Learn How to Read Body Language & Personality Types

Table of Contents

Introduction

"Can this person be trusted??"

"Does she really mean what she is saying?'

"What is their true intention?"

"Did they really commit the crime?"

We have all had those moments where we question everything around us. As is human nature, we get to interact with hundreds of people for different reasons, and the outcomes are always different. For instance, a very pretty lady or handsome man may approach you and stir some level of interest within you. The biggest determinant of how the interaction will proceed is dependent on the impression that they will make. You may also be a business owner seeking to hire a diligent and trustworthy person. Again, the person you select will undoubtedly be the one who will strike you like the most impressionable.

Human beings have one superpower. Our thoughts are hidden. Therefore, it is not a surprise that most people fall for a façade and only get to realize a person's true intention when it is too late. Often, you will hear the following statements from disgruntled persons:

"He/She changed. He wasn't like that when I met him"

"I can't believe person X would do this to me"

"Person Y was so kind and loving. I can't believe they committed the crime"

Often, it always comes down to the feeling of betrayal. I am sure that you have had instances where you misjudged a person's true intentions and ended up regretting trusting them. If you can be more honest, there are potentially instances where you had to put up an act to get something, e.g. lying at an interview to get a job or lying to your parents to avoid getting in trouble.

So, is there a way you can analyze someone to know their true intention or predict their actions?

Yes. There are a number of techniques and methodologies that have been developed by stellar psychologists over the years that help in the analysis of individual persons. These techniques are used in a wide range of scenarios such as solving crimes and determination of court case verdicts. There is literally no limit to the use of the skills and there can be applicable in any human interaction.

Notably, learning the art of analyzing people can save you a lot of problems in your personal and social life. If most people had the slightest knowledge of this subject matter, they would not interact with half the people that you are interacting with in the current day. Luckily, you are a step closer to learning human behavior and analysis strategies that will help you see people beyond their words.

Chapter One: Basics of Analyzing People

Many people are inclined to the belief that understanding people and what they really want is difficult. The fact that humans are capable of hiding their true intentions and thoughts supports this ideology, but only to a small degree. The truth is that human beings are the easiest to analyze due to the simple fact that we all tend to gravitate towards the same things.

If you ask most people what they would like to achieve most in this life, the following answers will be prevalent:

- Money

- Career development

- Talent growth

- Happiness

- Prestige

- Peace … etc.

Basically, we are all looking out for ourselves amidst a world which has very limited resources. The reason why you get up every day to work or study is all in an attempt to find your place in society and in the world, and you must realize that everyone is in the same race. Therefore, before you attempt to study or analyze someone, you must keep the following factors in mind:

There are Laws of Human Behavior

There are a number of pivotal laws that govern human behavior. Just like social sciences such as physics have laws, human behavior is not any different. Some of these laws include:

1. Human behavior is a unified system of investment, social influence, and justification

If you want to be successful in analyzing people, there is a need to be able to understand and explain what they are doing and why. For a long time, psychologists believed that the major determinant that governed any human behavior was the belief-desire framework. This ideology was inclined to the belief that any human action is instigated by desire. For example, if you get coffee, it is solely because you desire it.

Currently, there is a more sophisticated framework that is more scientifically-grounded, and that has received a wide accolade from psychologists, behaviorists, and other paradigms. This ideology is based on the discovery that there are three main processes that influence any human action. As an aspiring people analyst, it is up to you to determine the extent to which these three parameters affect any individual person.

The first process is **investment**. The term investment refers to the amount of work that has been directed towards something. When someone has deeply invested in something, it is an indication that they value that thing. Depending on the situation, you may be able to analyze such people from the value-association technique. To use the same example of a hiring manager, if a person has gone out of their way, prepared the necessary documents, and has strived to attain the highest level of education, you can positively conclude that they have attached some form of value to the career. Therefore, you can move on to the next analysis process having concluded whether they deserve a chance or not.

The second process is **Social influence**. Human beings are competitive by nature. It is for that reason that everyone is so inclined to becoming the best version of themselves so that they can stand out. Needless to say, society respects people who stand out and accords them social influence status that not everyone has. The more influence you have, the more prestige and in most cases, personal contentment. Everyone desires to be someone in society, and we cannot hold that against anyone. However, such quests have been known to influence people's behaviors and intent. If you can be able to predict these potential behaviors, you are well on your way towards successfully analyzing people

Finally, the third process is **justification.** This is the "why" in every action/reaction. Why do you want this job? Why do you love me? Why do you deserve this? In most instances, being able to accurately determine the "why" will give you an insight into a person's true intent.

Once you understand the three parameters, you will have better success in understanding and analyzing people. Just keep in mind that people are willing to go to whichever heights to get something once they believe that it will be a good addition in their lives, and you can tell the true intent by integrating the three processes.

2. There is an interrelation between Actions, Thoughts, and Feelings

Psychologists assert that there are three key interplays that govern individual human behavior. How we feel, think, and act. The three components influence each other. Our thoughts lead to what we feel, what we feel decides what actions we take.

Sounds complicated? Let's demystify them

An **action** is anything that can be observed by the physical eyes or is measurable using physiological sensors. If you want to really master the art of analyzing people, you must be an expert at interpreting actions. There is a popular adage that asserts that *"Actions speak louder than words"*. While a person may lie or attempt to be deceptive through words, how they really feel will always be evident through their actions. Note that, actions are not only comprised of the physical things that a person does but are also inclusive of aspects they cannot control such as muscular action and even activation of body functions such as sweat glands. It is for this reason that non-verbal cues (Chapter 3) are an imperative part of analyzing people.

Thoughts are the cognitive mental images that each person carries. According to me, thoughts are a superpower since nobody can access them. While many people may be inclined to believe that there is no way of telling what a person really thinks and their true intent, the truth is that thoughts are always manifested verbally and non-verbally. Once you know what to look for, you will always be able to read people's thoughts.

Feelings are emotions that present both conscious and subconsciously. In most cases, you can be able to age a person's true mental status by analyzing their emotions. Unlike words, which can be easily manipulated, feelings and emotions are very hard to fake. There are so many body processes that are governed by emotions such as the heart rate, respiration rate, muscular actions in various parts such as on the face and many more body functions. Once you know what to look for in a given situation, you will be able to accurately analyze them.

Actions, thoughts, and feelings are all connected. None of these emotions runs independently, and proper analysts look for telling signs concurrently. It is a fact that human beings are active consumers of sensory impressions, and it is all governed by the need to achieve what is considered to be good and avoiding any negatives. Therefore, you may want to first establish what you think a person really wants so that you can predict their actions and get to analyze what is real.

3. Behavioral Adaptations are all Darwinian Adaptations

As we stated earlier, human beings are always inclined towards actions that benefit them and put them on the trajectory to success. This behavioral adaptation has never been new, and it is well documented from time immemorial by philosophers such as Charles Darwin. The survival of the fittest has not changed one bit, and most people are motivated by contemporary factors such as money and prestige in the current times.

Once you understand that behavioral adaptations govern most of the people's acts and how they interact with others, you will be able to anticipate certain reactions. Also, you will have an easier time analyzing and getting credible inferences since you can actually see through words and what they claim to be true. Consider the following examples:

1.   We all know that we really cannot survive without money. To get the three basic needs; food, clothing, and shelter, money is paramount. Therefore, it is in the best interest of every human to put themselves in a position where they can earn the most to help live a robust life. So, if you are an interview or human resource manager conducting interviews, you cannot rely on verbal confirmation as anyone will do their best to convince you to hire them. Once you learn to look beyond the physical and study other human patterns, you will actually be at the forefront of finding the best person. Wouldn't you like that?

2.   Most immigration workers have less than 5 minutes to interview a person and make a decision on whether to grant them Visa's to different countries or not. With the short time allocated, most of these officials have robust training in analyzing people and they can gauge the true intention of an aspiring immigrant by just asking a few questions

As is clear in the two prompts, there is an actual need to analyze people on an in-depth basis so as to make credible inferences about what they truly stand for. There are hundreds of other occasions where a typical person would benefit from being able to analyze people, and they range from personal to professional situations.

The Key to Understanding Others is to Know Yourself

According to Socrates, knowing oneself is the beginning of wisdom. I agree.

The key to understanding others is to know yourself and what makes you tick. Once you fully understand who you are as a person, it becomes easier to know and analyze others.

There are a number of parameters that form the basis of knowing oneself as well as others. Always keep in mind that people are different, and you have to acknowledge that the inferences you will get from one person will be immensely different from what you get from another.

So, what is the most definite way of knowing yourself?

In the upcoming chapters, we will talk about the different methods and techniques for analyzing other people. Use all these techniques to know who you are first, and you may want to note down your discovery. Look back at your past experiences and how you responded to them, and write down the patterns. For example, what body language can you remember giving out when you were lying to someone? How do you react when you see someone that you love/hate? Some of the inferences are very uniform, which means that others will potentially react how you did too.

Understanding the Context is Vital

People may say a similar statement or showcase a particular non-verbal cue, and you would be wrong to make the same inferences about them. For example, after an accident, I expect the people involved to be totally shaken, regardless of whether they were at fault or not. The people may be shaking, unable to make eye contact, and look completely dazed from the beginning. Compare this to a person brought in for questioning, and when you ask them where they were on 22nd January they suddenly shift demeanor and start shaking. In the two cases, there are the same non-verbal cues, but the conclusions made are bound to be different.

Always Try to Establish a Baseline

If you have ever observed a person taking a lie-detector test, you will realize that the interviewer always begins by asking questions such as:

Is your name Jane?

Are you Female?

Are you wearing a red shirt?

Is today Monday?

These questions are basically those that a person has no business lying, and they are used to identify the baseline i.e., how a person behaves when they are relaxed and telling the truth. Most employment interviewers also begin by asking similar questions, and it helps them establish the baseline of both verbal and non-verbal cues. That way, when they move into the more intense questions, they can be able to detect changes in demeanor.

When you meet any person that you wish to analyze, you must be intent on getting the baseline from the word go. Regardless of whether you are meeting a person for a date or potential working relationship, it is imperative to know their baseline actions. Otherwise, you will have a lot of trouble analyzing them.

Always watch out for Signs in Clusters

The key to being a stellar analyzer is to watch out for signs in clusters. You must not concentrate on one part as that will both be weird to the other person and will not give you complete information. For example, do not concentrate on eye movements only. Watch the hands, proximity, tone and any other sign and begin establishing your conclusion from there.

Chapter Two: Identifying Different Personalities

One of the parameters used in the determination of who a person really involves a study of their individual personalities. Personality defines a person and determines most of their actions and patterns of thought. Analyzing people through the determination of their personality is, therefore, one of the most accurate techniques that you can ever employ due to one simple reason. People cannot hide who they are for long.

This analysis approach is suitable if you have the person around for a considerable amount of time. Most business owners usually employ a person on temporary basis/internship for at least 3 months before they decide whether to hire them on a permanent basis or not. During this time, most analyze a person's personality to see if they are a good fit.

Currently, there are many ways used to measure and determine the different personalities of different types of people. Five core traits have been identified and accepted as a credible determinant of people's personalities. These traits are:

Openness

People who fall under this category are known to be overly curious, open to adventure, and imaginative. Such people are also known to prefer rigid routines, and they are very high on pursuits of self-actualization and being open to different experiences. If a person falls under this category, there are a number of intense and euphoric experiences that they would go for such as living in a foreign place and undertaking artistic and relaxing techniques such as meditation. To the outside world, such people often appear to be unfocused and highly unpredictable.

To verify whether someone falls under this category, use the following checklist;

- Is the person open and willing to listen to multiple viewpoints from different people considering certain subject matters?

- Does the person seemingly seek new experiences and a lot of adventures?

- Does the person have a very creative way of expressing themselves?

- Is the individual open to a lot of variety and diversity?

- Does the individual score high on originality, insight, curiosity, and complexity?

- Does the individual have a high sense of aesthetic sensitivity?

- Does the individual have a high level of active imagination (Fantasy?)

If you ticked yes on all or a majority of the questions, then the person under analysis definitely falls in this category. As we stated, there are very many reasons why a person may be interested in carrying this analysis on others, key of which is to determine their suitability in a job environment.

If you are a hiring manager who works in a place where a strict routine is required, then people with this personality type may not be the best. While they may have all other credentials, there is a very high chance that they will always feel limited. Ultimately, such people may either quit on you or lose themselves completely. Good luck with making them come to work early.

On the other hand, there are a number of jobs where open people rank the highest, and these include travel companies and careers such as law, aviation, entrepreneurship, writing, graphic design, artists, and politicians.

You may also want to know a person's personality type to determine if they can be a good match for a romantic relationship. If you determine that your potential partner falls under this category, you can expect them to be highly agreeable and open to discussion and changes. A 2010 personality study involving 20,000 couples also revealed that couples who had one or all partners in this category displayed a high level of interpersonal trust, which resulted in very low levels of infidelity.

Basically, people who are open to experiences are always ready to live a more open and less traditional life, and they often do not have a need to conform to social statuses and expectations. So, if you conclude that a person has this personality, you know what to expect.

Conscientiousness

Individuals who have a conscientious personality are always highly organized and have a very strong sense of duty. Being the high organizers that they are, it all comes down to planning. In most cases, such persons can be considered to be the total opposite of the Open people. For example, while a person with an open personality can comfortably jet off to another continent with only a backpack, a conscientious person cannot. The latter must have planned to the tooth and you will likely find them with a very detailed analysis of how the trip will take place.

To determine if a person falls under this category, use the following checklist:

• Is the person ridiculously organized with everything well-planned out?

• Does he have difficulty leaving things undone?

• Does he have a very high level of self-discipline?

• Does he take appearance seriously and always want everything to be tidy?

• Can he be considered to be responsible and reliable?

• Is he cautious?

If you ticked off all or the majority of the questions, then you can conclude that the person is conscientious. Normally, many companies target these groups of people for various positions since they know that they will be assets. Conscientious people are very hard-working and goal-oriented, and their level of reliability is unmatched. The only disadvantage may be that you may need to look for an open person to be visionary and help come up with new ideas since the conscientious people largely follow protocol.

There is a number of careers that are great for conscientious people, and it includes medicine, managerial positions, freelance positions, and consultancy.

If you are looking for a romantic partner, choosing a person with a conscientious personality is highly advantageous. Not only will you be with a person who is organized both mentally and physically, but their persistence and responsibility will actually push you to do better.

Also, such people are less likely to get involved in any type of criminal activity due to their highly empathetic nature. To these people, taking unwarranted risks does not befit them. In the workplace, such people rarely get in trouble, which is good.

Extraversion

This is one of the most recognizable personality traits worldwide. An extrovert is also known as a social butterfly since they are chatty, very sociable, and mostly draw energy from crowds. The opposite of extroverts is introverted, and it consists of people who prefer to keep to themselves and avoid any social interactions. Note that, introversion does not amount to shyness but rather the preference of just being solo or involved in activities around small groups of people.

To know where someone lies on this spectrum, use the following checklist to check for levels of extroversion. If the person is the opposite, then you can conclude that they are introverted.

- Does the person like social gatherings?

- Do people say that the person is friendly and approachable?

- Does he always have a large group of friends around them?

- Does he like to talk things out, including their personal problems?

- Does he consider alone-time boring?

- Does he speak their mind?

- Does he display leadership skills?

- Is he vocal and seemingly always talking?

If your answer to the majority of the questions is yes, then the person under scrutiny is undoubtedly an extrovert. However, if the person is the total opposite, then you can conclude that they are introverts.

In careers and the work environment, extroverts are perfect for social roles that include leadership and tasks that need to be done by a team. Introverts, on the other hand, work best in individual tasks that do not require interactions and discussions with others.

When it comes to personal life and relationships, knowing your partner's character is the basis of a long and fruitful union. As is evident, the introvert-extrovert characters have very extreme differences, and failure of determining this early enough may just put your relationship in jeopardy. For example, while an introvert may choose to keep quiet and think during an argument, an extrovert may prefer to be more vocal about the issues and aim to solve them immediately. If you are in an extrovert-introvert relationship, the two of you will always have to find a middle ground that works for all.

Neuroticism

Neuroticism is characterized by a very high level of emotional instability. When a person lacks emotional stability, it means that they are highly unlikely to keep balanced and stable, and they may experience high tendencies of overreacting. Psychologists assert that most of the reactions experienced by neurotic persons are negative, which makes the people very unpleasant to others.

To know whether a person can be classified as neurotic, use the following checklist:

- Is the person volatile i.e., easily triggered?

- Is the person more susceptible to feelings such as stress, depression, and anxiety?

- Does the person seem to always be in a worry?

- Is the person super sensitive?

- Does the person have angry/hostile tendencies?

While the other personalities may take a little digging and observation to clearly manifest, people with neuroticism disorder are very hard to miss in any environment. In a typical workplace, there are always those people who people know are easily triggered and are very sensitive. Such people are likely to be very vocal about things such as people disrespecting them and just largely negative emotions. It only takes one statement for such people to be triggered, and you can never be too sure about how they will react. With such a personality, it goes without saying that such people rarely have many friends as they are always getting heated up with everyone.

It is very important to spot such people from the onset of any interaction, be it work or personal relationships. Knowing that a person is easily triggered will help you find ways of dealing/avoiding any instance that may result in a confrontation.

The laws of human behavior, as well as personalities, are all aspects that nobody really has control of. Scientists assert that some of these factors are genetic, and that is why some people just can't explain why they are easily triggered (neurotics), or why they live life on the edge (openness personas). It is just who they are.

When you begin analyzing people, there is always a need to first determine their personalities and factor in the laws of human behavior to avoid making erroneous judgments. In the subsequent chapters, we shall delve into the techniques and methodologies that will give us more accurate information about the person. The methods are quite popular and telling, and it is only when you factor in the person's personality that you will be more accurate as we shall see.

Chapter Three: Use and Power of Non-Verbal Communication

If you relied on verbal communication to analyze people, you would have hit a dead-end before you even begin. I have interacted with a lot of people for different purposes, and the one thing that I always ask is "tell me about yourself". If anyone has ever asked you that question, you agree with me that the first inclination is to give all your positive attributes. In most cases, the answers would be something like;

"I love dancing, cooking, adventure, learning..."

"I love working with people... I am a team-player... I am patient... I am tolerant..."

"I love children... working out...sports..."

The innate desire to be liked and accepted by others always drives us to seek gratification through such answers, and I have nothing against it. If you take a person's word for what they tell you,

you will always be disappointed. Luckily, psychologists and other experts know this only too well, and that is why when you tell them that "I am fine... I am not a drunkard... I am clean...", all they have to do is look at you and know that you are lying.

So, how do they do this?

Non-verbal cues. Nonverbal cues are one of the most powerful telling signs that psychologists and other bodies such as law enforcement officers use to solve cases. Whenever you hear that a person is being taken for questioning, the investigators already know that the person will potentially deny any wrongdoings. However, regardless of how much the person swears, cries, or tries to prove innocence, the investigators always know whether such persons are lying or not. Psychologists also use this super-power, and they almost always make credible judgments right after talking to someone.

Currently, non-verbal communication analysis has extended to almost all industries, and most trained interviewers are able to make accurate conclusions about a person just by speaking and observing various non-verbal cues. As Anivash Wandre once said, people may not always tell you how they feel but they will always show you[1]. Pay attention to what you see and you won't believe the inferences that you will deduce.

There are a number of non-verbal cues that you should pick up from the person that you are analyzing, and do not dismiss any as being trivial or unnecessary. Every little detail matters, and it will help you make the final judgement about a person. Some of the most critical non-verbal cues include:

Body Language Cues

Body language is one of the most telling non-verbal cues that instantly give away information. Avid analyzers such as psychologists and investigative lawmakers will tell you that they can be able to

---

[1] 37 Inspirational Quotes to Conquer Any Negativity in Your Life. (2019). Retrieved 16 November 2019, from https://www.cleverism.com/37-inspirational-quotes-to-conquer-any-negativity-in-your-life/

detect deceit or truthfulness based on the body language of their subjects. As we already concluded, words have little meaning since anyone can say anything to get certain outcomes. However, body language cannot be manipulated as much, and it will always tell the truth.

In a 2007 study that was conducted by professors from the communication and theatre association of Minnesota, results proved that 93 percent of all communication is actually non-verbal while only a measly 7 percent is verbal[2].

Many people often find it very hard to believe that body language can tell you the real intentions of a person for up to 93 percent accurately. It is important to note that most verbal communication is dependent on personal emotions, and human beings have learned the art of suppressing their true feelings due to multiple reasons. For example, when you are talking to a person with really bad breath, the first instinct may be to keep quiet and try to suppress your disgust as much as possible.

____

[2] Yaffe, P. (2019). The 7% rule. Retrieved 16 November 2019, from

You may even smile just to be polite and avoid saying anything so as to safeguard the feelings of the other person, but I can guarantee you that your body language will change.

There are a number of non-verbal cues that apply in multiple instances, and it is up to you to be keen to avoid missing a thing. The most telling signs include:

Facial Expressions

Before we get into facial expression and what the different cues mean, consider the following scenario:

FBI officials were looking into a high-profile crime, where a senior politician was murdered using a gun and stabbed using a sharp object. After much investigation, four suspects were taken into custody. As you would expect, all four denied committing the crime and insisted on their innocence. One after the other, the four suspects were questioned and grilled by forensic scientists and highly qualified CID officials. After two days, three had been released and one held as a key suspect. Sure enough, when all the investigations were over, the man was proven to be the murderer. When the officials were asked the point at which they knew that the man was the potential murderer, they revealed that his non-verbal cues were very telling.

At some point in the questioning, all men were asked the following yes/no questions:

"Did you shoot and stab the man on the chest?"

"Did you shoot and stab the man on the neck?'

"Did you shoot and stab the man on the thigh?"

All men answered "no" to these questions, very confidently. However, one of the suspects had a slight change of demeanor and looked down slightly when the agent asked about the thigh stab. He only looked up when the agent moved on to the next question. Instantly, the agents knew that he was a potential murderer, and it would only be a matter of time before they had more evidence on him.

Another key psychologist and stellar forensic scientist who analyzes people through nonverbal cues is Dr. Phil. Dr. Phil is undoubtedly a household name, and he has been responsible for helping solve hundreds of cases and airing them on his talk show. In a highly publicized episode, Dr. Phil managed to outline various timestamps of instances where the facial expression cues of one of his guests were very telling regardless of the fact his speech was the complete opposite.

The guest was being interviewed for catfishing allegations. When asked whether there were times he would forget to use the character voice and use his own, he made a contemptuous face as he stated that that would be a very rookie mistake that he would never do since he was an expert. Dr. Phil revealed that this is a facial expression that shows lack of empathy and arrogance. Evidently, the man was not sorry about what he had done.

The guest also made a rather telling face when he was asked whether he was in love with the man he had cat fished. With his eyes closed, his eyebrows were lifted while his face has a smirk at the side.

As soon as he made this face, Dr. Phil was certain that he was not remorseful, and that he had no regrets for what he had done and put an innocent person through. Despite the fact that he answered "Yes" to the question, the fact was that he never really cared for his victim since there was not an ounce of empathy in his demeanor.

The face is said to be the mirror of personality. There are very many studies that affirm that there is a very strong relationship between personality traits and facial features. Therefore, it is very important to keep all the personality information that we have learned in mind when you are studying people's facial expressions. Once you do so, you can accurately analyze a person and their intent with a high degree of precision.

So, what are the most telling facial expressions?

Eyes and Eye Movements

The eyes are said to be the windows to our soul and our thoughts. There is so much that you can tell just by looking at a person's eyes and the various movements that they make. Obviously, the reason why you will be so interested in decoding the meaning is the fact that humans will always hide their emotions depending on the different situations.

To be a stellar analyzer, follow the steps outlined below.

1.   The first thing that you need to **establish is your reason** for wanting to analyze someone. Do you want to know whether they are lying to you or trying to validate their authenticity? It doesn't matter if you are dealing with a stranger or not. The rules are the same.

2.   Once you establish your reason, the next step is **baselining the eyes**. Basically, the baseline process involves establishing how a person's eyes are behaving in a normal and non-threatening

situation. Do this by asking casual and neutral topics such as what they think about the weather, what they would like to drink, as well as movie and hobby preferences. The baselining questions should be no-brainers and something that nobody would really lie about. Take note of how the eyes behave as you are having this talk, and you have your baseline.

3.   The next step is looking for any **signs of eye deviation from the baseline**. For instance, if you are on a first date, you must keep tabs on the conversations and topics that make the other party's eyes deviate from the baseline. These are potential red-flags, and you may want to dig a little deeper. Psychologists and the FBI use this tactic all the time, and they are able to establish which questions they need to dig deeper on

In the case you realize any baseline deviations, take note of if it takes the form of:

Eye-blocking. Eye blocking often happens when a person feels threatened, or when they are repulsed by something that they see or hear.

Basically, this is an indication of a very uncomfortable situation, mostly due to disbelief or innate disagreement. Some people display eye blocking by rapid blinking while others take to rubbing the eyes using different forms. Learning to read eye-blocking can help you realize when you have repulsed people, enabling you to make it up or change the topic immediately.

Many years ago, I was out on a date with a person that I really liked and felt an instant chemistry. As we got to know each other, I may have said something demeaning about people who opted to go for a divorce rather than staying and fighting for their marriage. I was trying to come off as a keeper, and I missed his sudden change of demeanor which involved a lot of eye rubbing. Turns out, he had married young and had already been divorced once. Needless to say, we never went out for a second date. If I had known what I know now, I would have potentially saved the situation

Squinting. People will often squint their eyes if they do not like you or something that you are saying. This behavior is similar to eye-blocking, and you should address it quickly or clarify whatever it is that you have said before it gets worse.

Eye positions. Understanding eye positions is immensely important in the analysis process, and it will tell you a lot with the minimum effort.

You can analyze these eye movements when doing cross-examinations, interviews, or generally when a person is talking to you. From this analysis, you can tell whether a person is lying to you or not.

Right eye movements are associated with truth while left eye movements are associated with lies/making things up. You must realize that human beings will always have a strong desire to be liked and accepted, and sometimes creating a façade of who they seem like the best option. Regardless of the content through which you are analyzing a person, knowing this technique will help you know who you are really dealing with.

When a person is talking about a past event, they often rely on stored memories which they can vividly remember and describe. The memories are said to be on the left side of the brain, and that is why eye movements are to their upper left (Your right if you are directly facing them). However, if a person is just being deceptive and has to come up with a fake story, the eyes will shift to the left. The same case applies to when they are talking about remembered sounds such as conversations they claim to have had in the past.

When a person is having an internal dialogue/debate, they will most likely glance on the lower left. However, remembering a feeling will have them glance on the lower right

Note that, movement of eyes is considered to be one of the most accurate methods of analyzing a person/situation, although it is not fool-proof. You have to pay very close attention to the movements and put them in the context of the discussion to avoid making wrong judgments. In most cases, you have to associate the movement with the exact word or sentence that a person is saying. Consider the following scenario:

A person may be telling the truth about an incident and add bits of lies in between. For example, a statement like "I graduated in business and commerce from Harvard University" may have two parts. It may be true that indeed the person graduated in business and commerce, with the only exception being that they did not attend Harvard. If you are keen enough, you may notice the sudden shift in eye movements which will be red flags. If you are not sure about what you have observed, it is prudent to ask follow up questions at this point. For example, you can ask the person to tell you all about Harvard and what their experience was in the institution. Such a question requires a lengthy answer, and you will be able to observe eye movements much more accurately at this point.

Sideway glances. When a person is giving sideways glances, it is often an indication that they are uncertain, and often an indication of nervousness. You may want to ask follow up questions since this may be a sign of deception. Again, it really depends on the context of the conversation since most people are prone to make the sideways glances when they are withholding certain information. Maybe they just don't trust you.

In most cases, you will only make credible inferences when you understand what all the eye movements mean as well and connect then to the context of the conversation. Remember, if you are not sure, the best thing to do is to ask more follow up questions and analyze more signs.

Hand Gestures

People rarely realize how much their hand gestures speak for them. A CID officer once revealed how he knew that a person was lying through his hand movements. The man was accused of running a red light and hitting a pedestrian at a crosswalk right next to a junction. The man was very composed and his story relatively convincing. He argued that he was not the one since he has turned right at the junction while the pedestrian was hit on the left side of the junction. The CID officer noticed that whenever he sad that he had turned right, his hand gesture curved to the left. While everyone else was convinced, the officer insisted on his suspicion, and after much questioning the man finally broke and owned up.

When you are analyzing someone, watch out for these hand gestures:

No gestures. When a person is using no gestures at all and just has them sitting still throughout the conversation, it is a sign of indifference. Basically, they don't really care about the conversation, and you can be sure that they are withholding a lot of information from you.

Hands-on heart. A person will typically place his hands on his heart when saying statements such as "believe me", ``Trust me", "I swear". Basically, the gesture communicates their need to be accepted or believed. While most people may perceive this as a sign of sincerity, keep in mind that it does not amount to honesty. Such a person may only be interested in tuning you to believe them. The best thing at this point is to ask more follow-up questions.

Hands down with palm down. This is a sign of certainty. Therefore, there is a very high chance that the person is sure and truthful about what they are saying.

Palms facing each other with fingers touching. This is largely an indication that the person has vast expertise about what they are talking about. Most recruiters and human resource executives watch out for this sign when a person is describing their expertise in a subject matter.

Listing. Listing is usually done with the fingers when one is counting. For example, a person may show three fingers up when saying that they have three siblings. Often, hand movements tend to move faster than speech, and you are likely to catch a person lying at this point. For example, when a person says that they have three siblings but show two fingers, this is a red flag.

Open arms. When a person opens their arms in communication, it is often a sign of vulnerability that shows that they have nothing to hide. An honest person may make this gesture when they are being accused of something that they really did not do

Facepalm. This is a common gesture when someone hears something that they can't believe. If you are talking with someone and they make this gesture, you can be sure that you were out of line, and they were not impressed by what you said. You have the opportunity to rectify what you said immediately.

Air quotes. A person will use air quotes if they are being sarcastic, showing irony, or using a slang word. Depending on the context, you can decipher what this means and ask if you are not sure.

Clenched fist. When a person has their fist clenched, it is largely an indication that they are uneasy or angry.

Appearance

Appearance plays a very vital role in the development of first impressions. While we are really not supposed to judge a book by its cover, first impression results in what is known as the halo effect. Basically, this effect means that a person will expect more of what they strike from you from the onset. If you are wearing very good, neat clothes and you generally look attractive, people will expect more attractive attributes from you.

There are a number of instances where appearance plays a great role, and these include professional interviews, career expositions, and romantic meetings. In the first two, a desirable person is ideally the one with official, decent, and neutral-color clothes. The person must be very well-groomed. This is considered to be an indication of professionalism, and the person is considered to be more likely to perform well at the job. In the latter, a person wearing official clothes may be an indication that they are really not comfortable with you yet. However, when such people wear casual, bright, and comfortable clothing, it shows how comfortable they are with you.

Proxemics

Proxemics is defined as the distance between people. When you are talking to someone, analyzing their proxemics will help you determine whether they are drawn or repelled to you/the subject of discussion. Watch out for the following signs.

Maintaining distance. When a person maintains a relatively large distance and acts in a manner that suggests that they do not want to come closer, it is a sign of discomfort and to some extent mistrust. Depending on the context, you may want to do things that make the person feel more comfortable if you want to. In case you are having a conversation and the person leans back to create more distance, it may be an indication that they do not want to have that conversation, or that they are withholding something from you. Act accordingly by maybe asking more questions or following up using additional questions.

Closing in. If a person closes in to reduce the distance between you, it is largely an indication that they feel comfortable around you. Leaning forward in a conversation may also mean that a person is drawn to what you are talking about, and there is a high likelihood that whatever they are saying is honest.

If a person was closed in for a certain duration than suddenly leans back or moves back to create more distance, it could mean that they disagree with whatever you are saying or that they were offended by some aspects of the conversation. Clarity is always important, and you can ask them about it.

Common Myths about Body Language

It's evident that body language is one of the most telling signs that a person can use in the accurate analysis of another person. Most of the time, the body language and non-verbal communication cues that you pick are right, and trusting them will help you make credible inferences. That notwithstanding, it is imperative to learn about some of the most common myths that surround body language and non-verbal communication to help you to perfect your craft even more.

Myth 1: Liars don't make eye contact

This is one of the biggest myths that result in the wrong conclusion about a person. While it is true that some liars, children especially, may find it difficult making eye contact while lying, you must keep in mind that there are professionals out there. Conmen, narcissists, and other pathological liars know how to get their victim to trust them in entirety, and you can be sure that they will look at you in the eye as they spew out their lies without flinching.

The only problem with their strategy is their likelihood to overcompensate. Therefore, while a regular truthful person may just look at you briefly, liars will tend to look at you for longer to try and forcefully establish trust. If you notice someone using this strategy, hold your stare too and see how they react once they are done speaking. Some liars are bound to get nervous when you stare back without talking, and they may look down after finishing or continue "bluffing" unnecessarily.

Myth 2: Moving hands is a sign of uneasiness

Some people find it easier to express themselves using hand movements than using any other means. When a person moves their hands too much, it is not necessarily a sign that they are nervous. Rather, that may be just how they communicate with others.

Myth 3: You can tell what others are thinking by analyzing them

Analyzing people and their body language is not a superpower. You cannot be able to tell exactly what someone is thinking by looking at them. However, you can tell their emotions and catch any signs of deceit and lying. Therefore, do not expect to know people's thoughts by simply analyzing them. It will not happen.

Myth 4: Knowing analysis methods can help you to disguise yours

Most people who know all about analyzing others through the methodologies we have discussed think that they can disguise theirs. The major problem presented in this situation is that you will use a lot of conscious effort to disguise your feelings, prompting other body cues that can be picked by others. You can also tell when someone is trying to disguise their body language, and it is not possible for one to cover all of their tracks no matter how smart they are.

Chapter Four: Intuition

"Something told me that he couldn't be trusted"

"I had a very bad feeling when I went to meet them"

"I just had a feeling that he was a good person"

You have come across such words or uttered them yourself in the course of interacting with different people. Some people call it the sixth sense while others believe that it is the universe trying to tell them something. Whatever you call it, the fact remains that it is a very powerful basis and criterion that most people use in their decision-making processes.

The question is, how credible is this feeling and should you really rely on it to make decisions?

Intuition is one of the most underrated cognitive functions and the truth is that it is very effective and might be one of the most accurate analysis techniques that will help you to know all you want to about a person.

To understand the science and efficacy of intuition, we should understand the scientific aspect of it and how it works. Where exactly do the thoughts that amount to intuition emanate from?

The human brain has three divisions, the conscious, subconscious, and superconscious parts. The conscious part is the active part that we use in day-to-day decision making. For instance, if you decide to go for lunch at X hotel, you have made the decision with your conscious part of the brain. However, body functions such as breathing, putting one leg in front of the other to walk is all governed by the subconscious mind. If you bite your nails when you are nervous, you will agree with me that half the time you do not even know what you are doing. It just happens subconsciously.

The subconscious mind may seem like it is dormant but the truth is that it is one of the most powerful functionalities of the human body. People who follow the law of attraction can tell you just how powerful the subconscious mind is. Most of the power is derived from the fact that this brain part is wired to see patterns that the conscious mind does not. For example, when you are in deep thought and are walking home, you will just find yourself on the right road regardless of the fact that your conscious mind is preoccupied with other things.

The patterns are not limited, and the subconscious brain picks up patterns even when we are talking to other people. Every interaction, how to make you feel at the moment, and whether it ended happily or in a sad manner will all be stored deep in your memory. You may have met a person who made you feel a type of way through a particular way of interaction, and your relationship may have ended badly. You will lay in bed and think about this betrayal, analyzing what such people told you and trying to figure out how your relationship ended so badly. With time, you will get over it and "forget". The subconscious mind never forgets, and the pattern will be stored permanently.

After many years, you may meet another person who tells you similar things and just as you are about to fall for it again, you will get a bad feeling. It might not even occur to you that it is as a result of your past experience, but your body will just go into a defense mode which will prompt you to feel as though you need to take care. If you heed to that feeling, you may realize advantages later on. If you do not, you will potentially go against your intuition and when the bad outcome finally comes to pass, you will wish that you had listened to yourself.

In any particular minute, a million things are happening around us. The conscious mind cannot be able to pick up everything, and the deficit is picked up by the subconscious mind. You may be passing somewhere where someone is watching a documentary, and the two or three things that you pick will all be recorded in the subconscious. All these patterns and what most of the interactions made you feel will remain in the subconscious until you need them.

I am a believer in intuition or what most people call energies, and it has always worked to my advantage.

So, how do you use your intuition to be able to analyze people?

The first thing that you need to master is accessing your deeper consciousness. Intuitive people know the importance of slowing down time and accessing their inner thoughts through acts such as meditation and hypnotherapy. Self-awareness will increase your intuitive feelings, and all you have to do is be still, let go of your breathing, and listen to your breathing.

If this is not your cup of tea, it is okay. You can use the other methodologies discussed. However, if you read through the routines of most successful people such as Elon Musk, Will Smith, Oprah, Ellen DeGeneres, Steve Jobs, and many others, you will come to realize that they are very big on meditation and literally any practices that increase self-awareness. Steve Jobs was known to walk silently barefoot around his neighborhood whenever he was pondering a major change. Will Smith has a special meditation room where he spends time before taking on any major roles.

All these people will tell you that, when you are more aware, you can be able to pick up on the subtlest of signs that will influence your decision-making process. Professional poker players are very high on the use of intuition, and you should be too. When you have clarity about how you are feeling, your analysis will be more accurate, and you will avoid a lot of negative occurrences.

If you want to strengthen your intuition, I recommend two things:

- **Constant meditation.** Meditation simply involves sitting in a silent environment, letting go of all thoughts and just listening to your breathing. If you are having a hard time doing this, you may benefit more from guided meditation where an expert takes you through what to do step by step. There are so many sources of guided meditation audios online, and you can download them from credible sites such as YouTube. Download as many as you can, practice until you are finally able to do it on your own. You can also take on sports such as Yoga, and most of them have a guiding teacher that will tell you what to do and how to get into the meditation mode.

- **Connecting with nature.** This is the simplest practice, and all you have to do is talk a walk and force yourself to be conscious of everything around you. Walk barefoot on the grass and pay attention to how it glides under your feet. Touch sand and soil and pay attention to its texture and consistency. Smell the flowers, touch them and become fully indulged in the moment. You should not have any distractions such as phones with you, and you must pay attention to the wind, bird sounds, literally everything! The best time is so early in the morning before people wake up and fill the air with noise. If you have a garden in your background, the better for you.

Once you learn to strengthen your consciousness, the next thing is to pay attention to how people make you feel in the course of your interactions.

Some people call these energies, where they pay attention to whether a person is giving positive or negative energy. A person's talk really matters, as people who always see the bad in everything give off negative energies while people who try to see the good and handle disappointments well give off positive energies. Trust what people make you feel. This is who they really are.

Benefits of Intuition

1. Intuition adds to the list of analysis methodologies, and you will be able to **read people more**. For example, if a potential employer tells you that they will call you back, intuition will help you sense signs that will either affirm what the employer said or challenge it. If your intuition tells you that he is being honest, you can relax and wait for the call. If it tells you otherwise, it will help eliminate a lot of expectations, therefore enabling you to focus on other things.

2. Intuition largely **helps in cases that need caution**. Since the subconscious mind already has analyzed patterns and what comes of them, you will feel when something feels off. When you heed to it, you will potentially steer away from a situation that would have been really harmful, saving you from negative extremities.

3. Intuition will **help you make decisions in complex and unfamiliar situations**. When you are trying out a new thing, you will either hear voices urging you forward or telling you that you are making a mistake. Listen to these voices, and you will be able to make a more conclusive decision.

Once you become more conscious about everything around you, you can be sure that you will be able to pick people's personalities and non-verbal cues better.

Conclusion

It is evident that analyzing people is not as difficult as it seems. The techniques and methodologies outlined have been tested and proven to be absolutely imperative and beneficial in the analysis process. The one thing that you always need to keep in mind is that, establishing the baseline and distinguishing the context of the different conversations is quite imperative, as it determines the direction of the whole analysis process. Also, you have to keep practicing to perfect your analysis tact. Common sense is always of the essence, and you must never be too quick to jump to a conclusion. What is worse than jumping to conclusions is ignoring everything that you may have analyzed. If you are not sure, the major rule that applies is to carry out follow-up questions. In the whole process, do not be over-analytical and miss out on the moment. Subtlety will go a long way.

Bibliography

37 Inspirational Quotes to Conquer Any Negativity in Your Life. (2019). Retrieved 16 November 2019, from https://www.cleverism.com/37-inspirational-quotes-to-conquer-any-negativity-in-your-life/

Yaffe, P. (2019). The 7% rule. Retrieved 16 November 2019, from http://doi.acm.org/10.1145/2043155.2043156